Seeing The Light
In Dark Times

10 Day Devotional

Seeing The Light In Dark Times
10 Day Devotional

Copyright © 2020 Marsha Kuhnley
Visit the author's website at Rapture911.com

All rights reserved. No part of the non-biblical text in this publication may be reproduced, distributed, or transmitted in any form or by any means, including photocopying, recording, or other electronic or mechanical methods, without the prior written permission of the publisher, except in the case of brief quotations embodied in critical reviews and certain other noncommercial uses permitted by copyright law.

The text of the World English Bible (WEBP) is in the public domain and may be copied freely.

Published by Drezhn Publishing LLC
PO BOX 67458
Albuquerque, NM 87193-7458

Cover Design by Drezhn Publishing LLC

Print Edition - April 2020
Second Edition

ISBN 978-1-947328-38-9

Unless otherwise indicated, all Scripture quotations are taken from the World English Bible (WEBP), a public domain translation of the Holy Bible.

Scripture quotations marked (NLT) are taken from the Holy Bible, New Living Translation, copyright © 1996, 2004, 2015 by Tyndale House Foundation. Used by permission of Tyndale House Publishers, Inc., Carol Stream, Illinois 60188. All rights reserved.

SEEING THE LIGHT
IN DARK TIMES

10 Day Devotional

Marsha Kuhnley

Introduction

I was inspired to write this devotional because our world and way of life changed quite suddenly with the coronavirus outbreak in early 2020. Most of us have never witnessed entire cities, states, and even countries shutdown because people are told to stay at home. Countless people have lost their jobs. The stock market took an unprecedented dive. Who knew the hottest commodity would be toilet paper? With everything that's happening, people are afraid and uncertain about the future. People are wondering why God allows things like this happen.

I can tell you with absolutely certainty that God is in control and he has a plan in all of this. I know it can be hard to see God's light in dark times. That's what this devotional is for. It'll answer your pressing questions about how to be saved, why God allows bad things to happen, and how to have peace in the midst of the darkness. It'll bring you comfort during this difficult time.

> But there shall be no more gloom for her who was in anguish. ... The people who walked in darkness have seen a great light. The light has shined on those who lived in the land of the shadow of death. (Isaiah 9:1-2)

In this devotional, each day you'll read a selection of Scripture that I've chosen that illustrates the biblical truths corresponding to the topic of the day. That's followed up by a brief explanation of the Scripture. Then comes the lesson and application in which I present you a key truth and a question to consider for the day. The daily reading ends with a prayer. I estimate it'll take you about five to ten minutes to read each day.

If this is your first devotional, I hope you come to love them as much as I do.

Day 1
Why God Allows Dark Times

Scripture Reading

For I consider that the sufferings of this present time are not worthy to be compared with the glory which will be revealed toward us. For the creation waits with eager expectation for the children of God to be revealed. For the creation was subjected to vanity, not of its own will, but because of him who subjected it, in hope that the creation itself also will be delivered from the bondage of decay into the liberty of the glory of the children of God. For we know that the whole creation groans and travails in pain together until now. Not only so, but ourselves also, who have the first fruits of the Spirit, even we ourselves groan within ourselves, waiting for adoption, the redemption of our body. (Romans 8:18-23)

Not only this, but we also rejoice in our sufferings, knowing that suffering produces perseverance; and perseverance, proven character; and proven character, hope; and hope doesn't disappoint us, because God's love has been poured into our hearts through the Holy Spirit who was given to us. (Romans 5:3-5)

For they indeed for a few days disciplined us as seemed good to them, but he for our profit, that we may be partakers of his holiness. All chastening seems for the present to be not joyous but grievous; yet afterward it yields the peaceful fruit of righteousness to those who have been trained by it. (Hebrews 12:10-11)

It is good for me that I have been afflicted, that I may learn your statutes. (Psalm 119:71)

In my distress I called on Yahweh, and cried to my God. He heard my voice out of his temple. My cry before him came into his ears. (Psalm 18:6)

Explanation

When Adam and Eve sinned in the garden, God's entire creation was cursed as a result. That's why there is sin, evil, sickness, and pain in the world. We live in a fallen world.

You must remember that the sufferings you experience today are only temporary. The Apostle Paul tells us they aren't even worthy of being compared to the wonderful things that await us in heaven.

This state of affairs we live in gives God the great opportunity to show us his love. That's what he wants you to think about when fear, suffering, heartache, or pain comes your way. God's love conquers fear. Think of God's love for you. If you have placed your faith in Jesus, your redemption is coming soon. Jesus is coming to rapture his church. You're going to get a new body. You're going to live with him forever one day. You have nothing to fear because nothing can take that away.

Paul also tells us that suffering produces perseverance which is the ability to persist, carry on, and endure despite hardship and opposition. This produces character. That's what makes you who you are. Can you think of someone who persevered despite the immense pain and suffering? It's Jesus! He knows all about living in darkness. When he was crucified, darkness covered the land and he cried out to God, "Why have you forsaken me?" That's because when God placed all of your sins and the sins of everyone else upon him, God departed from him. Jesus knows what it's like to live in dark times.

It's Jesus's character that you prove you have when you're able to keep going when darkness surrounds you. Your experience will help you not only relate to Jesus, but to others who are going through something similar. Then you'll be able to comfort others and help them during their time of need. And why do you press on? It's because you have hope. You trust in all of God's promises. And the more you continue to stand firm, the more faith and hope you develop.

Another reason God allows dark times is because it's one of God's divine tools of discipline. He uses it to draw people to him so he can then comfort, correct, and teach. Sickness and tragedy get people thinking of their own morality, life after death, and God. You've likely searched through the Bible for answers and encouraging words. That's exactly what he wants people to do. When you reach out to God during your dark time, know that God is there and he's listening.

Lesson

Would you long for heaven and your new body if life on earth was already like life in heaven? Consider Jesus's words that it's difficult for a rich man to enter heaven. That's because they don't see their need for a savior. Dark times point to Jesus, the light of the world, and the savior of mankind.

Application

Today, cry out to God for help during the dark time you're facing. Read your Bible and draw close to God. Pour out your heart to him. Tell him about all of your fears, anxieties, pain, sorrow, doubt, sickness, and struggles. He already knows what you're going through, but he longs for you to unburden yourself. So, pour everything that's weighing you down onto God. He will give you his peace in return. Then remember God's promises for believers and be filled with hope.

Prayer

Dear God, it's hard living in dark times. It's scary. I worry about many things and doubt your promises. Please forgive me. I ask that you take all of my burdens and give me your promise of peace in return. I pray that you help me persevere through the darkness so I can develop proven character that will enable me to relate to others and help them when their need arises. Please console my family and friends and help them seek you too. I pray that the people I care about who don't know you yet come to trust in you. Help me turn on the light, draw closer to you in this dark time, and receive comfort in your words and promises.

Day 2
Live In The Light

Scripture Reading

In the beginning was the Word, and the Word was with God, and the Word was God. The same was in the beginning with God. All things were made through him. Without him, nothing was made that has been made. In him was life, and the life was the light of men. The light shines in the darkness, and the darkness hasn't overcome it. ... The Word became flesh and lived among us. We saw his glory, such glory as of the only born Son of the Father, full of grace and truth. (John 1:1-5, 14)

Again, therefore, Jesus spoke to them, saying, "I am the light of the world. He who follows me will not walk in the darkness, but will have the light of life." (John 8:12)

Now I declare to you, brothers, the Good News which I preached to you, which also you received, in which you also stand, by which also you are saved, if you hold firmly the word which I preached to you—unless you believed in vain. For I delivered to you first of all that which I also received: that Christ died for our sins according to the Scriptures, that he was buried, that he was raised on the third day according to the Scriptures, and that he appeared to Cephas, then to the twelve. Then he appeared to over five hundred brothers at once, most of whom remain until now, but some have also fallen asleep. Then he appeared to James, then to all the apostles, and last of all, as to the child born at the wrong time, he appeared to me also. (1 Corinthians 15:1-8)

How precious is your loving kindness, God! The children of men take refuge under the shadow of your wings. They shall be abundantly satisfied with the abundance of your house. You will make them drink of the river of your pleasures. For with you is the spring of life. In your light we will see light. (Psalm 36:7-9)

Explanation

In order to see in the dark, you need to turn on a light and then use it to light your way. Jesus Christ is the "Son of the Father," which is God, the "Word," and the "light of the world." What's more is that Jesus is God in the flesh. We learn that in the Scriptures that say "the Word was God" and the "Word became flesh." That's right, God stepped out of heaven and came to earth. His mission—conquer darkness.

You see, you're a sinner. In fact, we're all sinners and as such we deserve death and darkness in hell because we've disobeyed God. We're not pure and holy like God. That's a problem because that means we can't live in heaven where God lives. But there's great news! God loves us so much that he willingly died to save us. He wants all of us to live with him for eternity. All we have to do is believe.

Believe that Jesus is who he says he is, that he was crucified for your sins, that he rose from the dead since he's God and all powerful, and that afterwards he appeared to many people, including Paul the Apostle who wrote that account.

Once you believe, Jesus fills you with his Holy Spirit and lives inside of you. Yes, the light of the world is truly within you. You'll no longer be destined to live in eternal darkness. With Jesus inside of you, you won't focus on the dark times any longer. You'll see the light instead because that's what you're filled with and where you're destined to live. Your fear will be replaced with love and peace. Your sorrow and despair will be replaced with hope. You'll see God's loving kindness through it all. You'll fix your eyes on Jesus and where he lives, heaven.

Jesus conquered death and darkness when he stepped out of the tomb. This dark time will not conquer you either. Follow Jesus. Trust in his promises. Know that he's won. The darkness lost and has no power over you. You have the light of life because Jesus, who is the light, lives inside of you.

Lesson

During this dark time, have you grabbed the light and turned it on? You must grab ahold of Jesus and accept him as your personal savior in order to conquer sin, evil, and the darkness. If you've done that, then you need to be walking with Jesus, who is the light, every single day. Otherwise, you'll be walking away from Jesus out into the darkness.

Application

Today, realize everything that Jesus has done to save you from the darkness. Pray to accept him into your heart and be filled with relief. Seeing Scripture come to life is very powerful, especially when we're overwhelmed with fear and uncertainty. Watch a movie about Jesus this week. My personal favorites are *The Passion of the Christ*, *Son of God*, and *Risen*. There's also the timeless *The Jesus Film*, which is free to watch online and available in hundreds of languages. Experience Jesus in a way that perhaps you haven't before or haven't in a long time. You'll meet Jesus if you don't know him yet. It'll help you see the light and it'll inspire you to walk with him in his light.

Prayer

Dear God, thank you for coming to earth as a human with flesh and blood and then shedding your blood to save me from my sins. I believe that Jesus is the Son of God, that he's God in the flesh, that he died for my sins, and that he rose from the grave and reigns in heaven. I don't want to live in the darkness and be afraid any longer. Please forgive me for being a sinner. I want Jesus to come into my life and fill me with his light. Please help me read my Bible, pray, and thus walk with Jesus every day.

Day 3
Have Peace In The Darkness

Scripture Reading

David said to Solomon his son, "...Don't be afraid, nor be dismayed, for Yahweh God, even my God, is with you. He will not fail you nor forsake you." (1 Chronicles 28:20)

"Don't let your heart be troubled. Believe in God. Believe also in me. ... If I go and prepare a place for you, I will come again and will receive you to myself; that where I am, you may be there also." ... Jesus said to him, "I am the way, the truth, and the life. No one comes to the Father, except through me. ... I will pray to the Father, and he will give you another Counselor, that he may be with you forever: the Spirit of truth, whom the world can't receive, for it doesn't see him and doesn't know him. You know him, for he lives with you and will be in you. ... But the Counselor, the Holy Spirit, whom the Father will send in my name, will teach you all things, and will remind you of all that I said to you. Peace I leave with you. My peace I give to you; not as the world gives, I give to you. Don't let your heart be troubled, neither let it be fearful." (John 14:1, 3, 6, 16-17, 26-27)

"I have told you these things, that in me you may have peace. In the world you have trouble; but cheer up! I have overcome the world." (John 16:33)

In nothing be anxious, but in everything, by prayer and petition with thanksgiving, let your requests be made known to God. And the peace of God, which surpasses all understanding, will guard your hearts and your thoughts in Christ Jesus. (Philippians 4:6-7)

Behold, a violent storm came up on the sea, so much that the boat was covered with the waves; but he was asleep. The disciples came to him and woke him up, saying, "Save us, Lord! We are dying!" He said to them, "Why are you fearful, O you of little faith?" Then he got up, rebuked the wind and the sea, and there was a great calm. The men marveled, saying, "What kind of man is this, that even the wind and the sea obey him?" (Matthew 8:24-27)

Explanation

Jesus, God in the flesh, is always with you. His love for you conquers the darkness and the fear it brings. If you've put your faith in him, he will not remove his Holy Spirit from you. He will not renege on any of his promises. You don't need to worry or be afraid of those things.

You have the power to control your thoughts. Jesus commanded you to not be afraid or troubled. That means he's given you the power to conquer those feelings. The Holy Spirit is your guardian. He guards your heart and mind. He brings you peace. He teaches you all things. If you've put your faith in Jesus, then the Holy Spirit will use God's word to protect your thoughts and bring you comfort in dark times.

The key to conquering the anxiety that the darkness wields is prayer and thanksgiving. You just need to unburden yourself of what troubles you, what brings you grief, and what you need. God will take all of those concerns and pain and give you his peace in return. However, don't forget the element of thankfulness. Thank God for the Holy Spirit and for taking your darkness and giving you his light.

Regardless of what's happening in your life, the life of a loved one, or in the world, know that God is in complete control. He controls the storm, the darkness, and the trial you're experiencing. He will rebuke the storm when it's time, when it's fulfilled its purpose. In the midst of the dark storm, Jesus wanted his disciples to have faith. That's what's required of you too. Let this dark time grow your faith.

Increase your faith by trusting in God's promises. You know, Jesus told you what the future holds so that you would have peace. He wants you to believe. He gave you promises so that you could hold onto them during times like this.

One of those exciting promises is that Jesus is coming back to get us. This is the rapture of his church, the people who've put their faith in him for salvation. We're living in the last days, so it could happen any minute. Let that put a smile on your face. Today could be the day that you see Jesus face to face.

Lesson

Have you placed your faith in Jesus? Then you have the Holy Spirit living inside of you who provides God's peace.

Have you told God what's on your mind and troubling you? You have to give all of your fear and anxiety away to Jesus so that he can fill you up with the cure that conquerors those feelings, his love and peace.

Are you growing your faith during your dark time by recalling God's promises? You must know his promises in order to hold onto them.

Application

Today, accept Jesus into your life and receive his Holy Spirit if you haven't yet. You can't achieve peace. It has to be given to you by the author of peace, Jesus. Unburden yourself by telling Jesus everything that troubles you. Then stop focusing on your darkness. Instead look to God's promises. Find at least one promise in the Bible that you can grab ahold of this week. Keep it in your heart and recall it when the darkness tries to creep back in.

Prayer

Dear God, help me realize that my attempts to bring order out of chaos and manufacture my own peace will not work. I want to trust in your promises. Since I have placed my faith in Jesus, I know that the Holy Spirit lives inside of me. I ask that you take away everything that troubles me and let the peace that the Holy Spirit provides guard my thoughts instead. Help me trust in and recall your promises when the darkness comes up me.

Day 4
Be A Prayer Warrior

Scripture Reading

When he finished praying in a certain place, one of his disciples said to him, "Lord, teach us to pray, just as John also taught his disciples." He said to them, "When you pray, say, 'Our Father in heaven, may your name be kept holy. May your Kingdom come. May your will be done on earth, as it is in heaven. Give us day by day our daily bread. Forgive us our sins, for we ourselves also forgive everyone who is indebted to us. Bring us not into temptation, but deliver us from the evil one.' " He said to them, "Which of you, if you go to a friend at midnight and tell him, 'Friend, lend me three loaves of bread, for a friend of mine has come to me from a journey, and I have nothing to set before him,' and he from within will answer and say, 'Don't bother me. The door is now shut, and my children are with me in bed. I can't get up and give it to you'? I tell you, although he will not rise and give it to him because he is his friend, yet because of his persistence, he will get up and give him as many as he needs. I tell you, keep asking, and it will be given you. Keep seeking, and you will find. Keep knocking, and it will be opened to you. For everyone who asks receives. He who seeks finds. To him who knocks it will be opened." (Luke 11:1-10)

And take the helmet of salvation, and the sword of the Spirit, which is the word of God; with all prayer and requests, praying at all times in the Spirit, and being watchful to this end in all perseverance and requests for all the saints. (Ephesians 6:17-18)

In the same way, the Spirit also helps our weaknesses, for we don't know how to pray as we ought. But the Spirit himself makes intercession for us with groanings which can't be uttered. He who searches the hearts knows what is on the Spirit's mind, because he makes intercession for the saints according to God. (Romans 8:26-27)

In nothing be anxious, but in everything, by prayer and petition with thanksgiving, let your requests be made known to God. (Philippians 4:6)

Explanation

We've previously talked about the importance of praying in order to conquer the darkness. In today's reading, you learned how to pray. Jesus's disciples didn't know how to pray and when they asked him, he gave them clear instructions to follow. Now, you can certainly pray the exact prayer that Jesus used in his example, however, it's meant to be a template, not something you blindly repeat every day.

The components of a good prayer include praise to God, prayer for others, prayer for God's will to be done, prayer for your own needs, a recognition of your sins and a petition for forgiveness, and prayer to keep yourself away from temptation. It's especially important that you remember to pray for other believers. "The saints" is how Paul the Apostle described them. Every prayer of yours doesn't need to include all of those things, but some certainly should.

I want you to notice that in Jesus's example when he prayed for his and his disciples needs, he asked for "daily bread." He didn't ask for something they wanted, like maybe a bus so they wouldn't have to walk everywhere. He didn't ask for a year's supply of food so they didn't have to work so hard every day. No, he just asked God to provide nourishment for them each day.

Another key truth in those Scriptures is to be persistent in your prayers. You should pray at all times and never give up. It's about perseverance. So pray in the morning when you're starting your day, pray during the day as the need arises or when you want to thank God for helping you, and pray at night to hand your burdens over to God and then sleep well with God's peace.

Perseverance means you keep praying even in the face of opposition, like disappointment. Just because you don't see progress happening doesn't mean God isn't listening. Remember the prophet Daniel prayed and it took weeks for an angel to get to him with an answer because he was held up in spiritual warfare. Keep praying for the salvation of your loved ones. Remember that God loves them even more than you do and wants to see them saved.

For the times we find it difficult to pray because we can't find the right words, or we don't even know what to ask for, take comfort in knowing the Holy Spirit has your back. The Holy Spirit is always interceding, that means praying, on your behalf. What's more is that the Holy Spirit's prayers are always in line with God's will in your life.

Lesson

We're in a spiritual war and one of our weapons is prayer. Are you a prayer warrior?

Jesus gave us the perfect example of a prayer. When you pray to God, do your prayers include all the elements that he had?

God wants us to be persistent in our prayers. Is there something you stopped praying about that you need to start petitioning God for once again?

Application

Today, become a prayer warrior. Say a prayer to God that has all of the elements in Jesus's example. Then think of all the believers in your life and say a prayer for them. Pray for your family, friends, and your pastor. Pray that God provides for them, that God keeps them away from temptation, and that God's will for them is accomplished. For the days you struggle to know what to pray, go to a Psalm or find the lyrics to a favorite Christian song and use that to guide your prayer.

Prayer

Dear God, please help me become a prayer warrior today. Help me make prayer not just a daily habit, but a throughout the day habit. I pray Psalm 23 for myself, my loved ones, and my pastor.

Yahweh is my shepherd; I shall lack nothing. He makes me lie down in green pastures. He leads me beside still waters. He restores my soul. He guides me in the paths of righteousness for his name's sake. Even though I walk through the valley of the shadow of death, I will fear no evil, for you are with me. Your rod and your staff, they comfort me. You prepare a table before me in the presence of my enemies. You anoint my head with oil. My cup runs over. Surely goodness and loving kindness shall follow me all the days of my life, and I will dwell in Yahweh's house forever. (Psalm 23:1-6)

Day 5
Pray For Healing

Scripture Reading

Is any among you suffering? Let him pray. Is any cheerful? Let him sing praises. Is any among you sick? Let him call for the elders of the assembly, and let them pray over him, anointing him with oil in the name of the Lord; and the prayer of faith will heal him who is sick, and the Lord will raise him up. If he has committed sins, he will be forgiven. Confess your sins to one another and pray for one another, that you may be healed. The insistent prayer of a righteous person is powerfully effective. (James 5:13-16)

Trust in Yahweh with all your heart, and don't lean on your own understanding. In all your ways acknowledge him, and he will make your paths straight. Don't be wise in your own eyes. Fear Yahweh, and depart from evil. It will be health to your body, and nourishment to your bones. (Proverbs 3:5-8)

Have mercy on me, Yahweh, for I am faint. Yahweh, heal me, for my bones are troubled. My soul is also in great anguish. But you, Yahweh—how long? Return, Yahweh. Deliver my soul, and save me for your loving kindness' sake. ... Yahweh has heard my supplication. Yahweh accepts my prayer. (Psalm 6:2-4, 9)

Levi made a great feast for him in his house. There was a great crowd of tax collectors and others who were reclining with them. Their scribes and the Pharisees murmured against his disciples, saying, "Why do you eat and drink with the tax collectors and sinners?" Jesus answered them, "Those who are healthy have no need for a physician, but those who are sick do. I have not come to call the righteous, but sinners, to repentance." (Luke 5:29-32)

Don't be afraid of the things which you are about to suffer. Behold, the devil is about to throw some of you into prison, that you may be tested; and you will have oppression for ten days. Be faithful to death, and I will give you the crown of life. (Revelation 2:10)

Explanation

Pray. That's the key truth in today's reading. If you're suffering or sick, God wants to hear your prayer. That's because God wants you to draw close to him and realize that you need him. He has the power to heal you if it's in his will.

God also doesn't want you fighting your battle alone. He wants you to get the church leaders and your friends to pray for you too. I know this can be difficult during a time like the present in which the coronavirus is keeping us all at home or quarantined. Call your church and tell them of your prayer need, submit a prayer request online, or post one to your social media page instead.

Sometimes sickness is brought on because of sin. It's God's discipline to help you repent. If you've committed a sin that you haven't confessed to God, do that so God can forgive you, give you his peace, and heal you if that's his will. If you've sinned against someone else, ask for their forgiveness too.

Yet, other times suffering is about withstanding God's test of faith. Remain faithful to God during your dark time. Don't curse God or renounce him. If you remain faithful, even to the point of death, then God promises a crown of life to you because of your faith. We don't like to think of God allowing bad things to happen to us, but sometimes he does because he has a reward waiting for us on the other side. Think of God's blessing in the midst of your pain.

We also learned today that not all sickness is physical. If you don't have a personal relationship with Jesus, then you have a spiritual sickness. Unrepentant sin leads to eternal death and darkness. Jesus is the physician for that. His treatment is simple and easier than taking a pill. Just believe that Jesus is the Son of God, that he died for your sins, that he didn't stay dead, but was resurrected, and reigns in heaven today.

Whatever darkness you are faced with today, trust in God and not in yourself and your own understanding. You must realize that God is the author of all creation. He wrote the entire story already. You don't know everything that God has in store for the future. You are just living through one page at a time. Take comfort in knowing that God hears your prayer for healing, and he accepts it. Keep praying because persistent prayer is an effective cure.

Lesson

We must pray to God for healing and request that our church leaders and loved ones pray for us too. If you are sick or suffering, have you prayed to God for healing? Have you asked your church, family, and friends to pray for you?

Do you know someone who is sick and needs healing, either physical or spiritual healing? Then pray for that person every day.

Have you confessed your sins to God and asked for forgiveness? Confess to him and apologize to your friends and family if you need to. Then trust that God will physically heal you if that's what he wills for you.

Application

Today, commit to praying to God for healing. Whether it's for yourself or for a loved one and whether it's for physical or spiritual healing. Be that righteous person with insistent prayer that James wrote about and know that your prayer is heard by God and is making a difference.

Prayer

Dear God, I pray for healing for myself and for my friends and family. Please forgive me of my sins so that I can be healed. I know that your word says Jesus was sent to heal the brokenhearted. I believe and trust that if you desire to heal me, then I will be healed. However, I also know that this dark time may be a time of testing for me. Please help me remain faithful and in constant prayer to you. Help me fix my eyes on Jesus and the treasure which awaits me when the light shines on this dark time.

Day 6
Fill Your Soul With Light

Scripture Reading

For those who live according to the flesh set their minds on the things of the flesh, but those who live according to the Spirit, the things of the Spirit. For the mind of the flesh is death, but the mind of the Spirit is life and peace. (Romans 8:5-6)

If then you were raised together with Christ, seek the things that are above, where Christ is, seated on the right hand of God. Set your mind on the things that are above, not on the things that are on the earth. For you died, and your life is hidden with Christ in God. ... Put to death therefore your members which are on the earth: sexual immorality, uncleanness, depraved passion, evil desire, and covetousness, which is idolatry. ...But now you must put them all away: anger, wrath, malice, slander, and shameful speaking out of your mouth. Don't lie to one another, seeing that you have put off the old man with his doings, and have put on the new man, who is being renewed in knowledge after the image of his Creator.... Put on therefore, as God's chosen ones, holy and beloved, a heart of compassion, kindness, lowliness, humility, and perseverance; bearing with one another, and forgiving each other, if any man has a complaint against any; even as Christ forgave you, so you also do. Above all these things, walk in love, which is the bond of perfection. (Colossians 3:1-3, 5, 8-10, 12-14)

While we don't look at the things which are seen, but at the things which are not seen. For the things which are seen are temporal, but the things which are not seen are eternal. (2 Corinthians 4:18)

Finally, brothers, whatever things are true, whatever things are honorable, whatever things are just, whatever things are pure, whatever things are lovely, whatever things are of good report: if there is any virtue and if there is anything worthy of praise, think about these things. Do the things which you learned, received, heard, and saw in me, and the God of peace will be with you. (Philippians 4:8-9)

Day 6 – Fill Your Soul With Light

Explanation

"You are what you eat" isn't just true of food and your physical body. It's also true about what you feed your soul. What you consume has an effect on your spiritual health too.

After you put your faith in Jesus and become a believer, you are born again. That means you're a new person. So, the first thing you need to do is stop sinning. Paul the Apostle lists a whole bunch of sins that need to be put away including sexual sins, coveting which means you want what other people have, idolatry which is worshiping anything other than God, being angry, speaking evil of other people, and lying. That's what defined your old self and your sinful life. That's not you anymore.

The new you is compassionate and kind. You persevere, bear with and forgive other people, and most of all you love. You have all the fruits of the Spirit which include love, joy, peace, patience, kindness, goodness, faith, gentleness, and self-control. Your old self is dead.

Since you love other people and Jesus most of all, then you can't bear to do anything that would hurt or wrong them. You wouldn't think of sinning against them. That's what walking in love is all about. You obey God with all your heart. You desire to know him more and more each day. You want other people to know and love Jesus just as much as you do.

Once you've conquered sinful actions, you need to battle your dark and sinful thoughts. Yes, your thoughts can be sinful. If your mind is full of fear or worry, then you are doubting God's love and promises. If you're angry with God or yourself because of the dark time you're going through, you're one step away from physically expressing that anger to people you love, and you're fighting against what God has done.

The cure is to stop thinking about the darkness. Think about the light instead. Think about heavenly things, good things, things that are worthy of God's praise. Doing that will bring you life and peace. Your life will be a reflection of the things you think about. If you think about God's love and promises, your faith with grow, you'll show God's love, and those dark thoughts will be crowded out and disappear.

Lesson

Have you cast away your old sinful self and the behaviors you used to do? You must put on your new self and do everything with God's love in mind.

What are you filling your soul with? You must conquer your dark thoughts by thinking of heavenly things, things that Jesus would approve of. That means you need to be mindful of not only what you think about, but what you watch, listen to, and read as well.

Application

Today, you are going to conquer the darkness that plagues your mind. Choose today to stop watching TV shows that aren't good for your soul. You know which ones they are. They're full of violence, cursing, and sex. I know it's going to be hard, but you can do it because you love Jesus. It doesn't matter how those stories end. Your soul is more important than that, isn't it? Choose today to stop listening to music that's full of hateful or sinful lyrics. Listen to something that will lift up your spirits instead. Choose today to learn more about heaven. Randy Alcorn's book, *Heaven*, is an excellent place to start.

Prayer

Dear God, thank you for giving me the tools necessary to combat the dark thoughts that wreak havoc in my mind. Help me to turn away from a life of sin and turn toward you and lead a life filled with love. Love for you and for others. Help me purge the TV shows and music that aren't good for me. I want to think of good and heavenly things from now on. I pray for your peace and light to fill my mind.

Day 7
Be A Friend

Scripture Reading

For where two or three are gathered together in my name, there I am in the middle of them. (Matthew 18:20)

They continued steadfastly in the apostles' teaching and fellowship, in the breaking of bread, and prayer. (Acts 2:42)

Let's consider how to provoke one another to love and good works, not forsaking our own assembling together, as the custom of some is, but exhorting one another, and so much the more as you see the Day approaching. (Hebrews 10:24-25)

However you did well that you shared in my affliction. You yourselves also know, you Philippians, that in the beginning of the Good News, when I departed from Macedonia, no assembly shared with me in the matter of giving and receiving but you only. For even in Thessalonica you sent once and again to my need. Not that I seek for the gift, but I seek for the fruit that increases to your account. (Philippians 4:14-17)

Now when Job's three friends heard of all this evil that had come on him, they each came from his own place: Eliphaz the Temanite, Bildad the Shuhite, and Zophar the Naamathite; and they made an appointment together to come to sympathize with him and to comfort him. When they lifted up their eyes from a distance, and didn't recognize him, they raised their voices, and wept; and they each tore his robe, and sprinkled dust on their heads toward the sky. So they sat down with him on the ground seven days and seven nights, and no one spoke a word to him, for they saw that his grief was very great. (Job 2:11-13)

And above all things be earnest in your love among yourselves, for love covers a multitude of sins. Be hospitable to one another without grumbling. As each has received a gift, employ it in serving one another, as good managers of the grace of God in its various forms. (1 Peter 4:8-10)

Explanation

God says he's with you when you gather with at least one other person in his name. This is great news for those of us who can't attend church in person because we have to stay at home and distance ourselves socially from other people, all because of the coronavirus. Technology enables us to gather virtually with other believers anywhere in the world.

You see, God wants you to be friendly. He doesn't want you to be a hermit and live life by yourself, even when there's a virus. That's because there's a purpose in gathering together that he doesn't want you to miss out on. The early church learned together, hung out together, ate meals together, and prayed together. They also encouraged each other to love and do good things.

These are all important things when we're living in and going through dark times. You need other people to help you through it. They can offer support and prayer. In truly difficult times, your family and friends can be like Job's friends. Job was so grieved that they didn't know what to do or say to comfort him, but that was okay. They showed up, they cried with him, and they sat with him. Their presence was enough.

Sharing in other people's afflictions is what Paul the Apostle encouraged. Give to those who are in need. God has given each of us spiritual gifts which include: the ability to give good advice, to share knowledge, faith, healing, performing miracles, discerning spirits, speaking in languages, interpreting languages, serving, teaching, encouraging, giving, and leading. He wants you to use the gifts he's given you to serve others.

Did you notice it doesn't have to be money? The gift of giving was only one of many. You can share in people's affliction with your time, your comfort, your encouragement, and even with your prayers for healing. Just like Job's friends, your presence and willingness to help is what's important.

For those who are friendly and hospitable, there's fruit that awaits you in heaven. When we give our God given gifts away, we get God's gift of heavenly treasure in return.

Lesson

Be involved, be present, and be a friend for someone during this difficult and dark time. Who are you a friend to?

Consider the things you are passionate about and good at so that you can identify your spiritual gifts. Have you put those skills to use for the friend you've identified?

If you're unable to attend church or fellowship with other people in person, are you staying connected in other ways and using technology to help you? It's important to stay socially connected even when we must be physically distant.

Application

Today, identify who you are a friend to. It can be your family members, friends, fellow church members, your neighbor, or even a co-worker. Choose to connect with at least one of them today. Encourage them during this dark time. Find out how you can pray for them and then commit to praying for them this week. Use your spiritual gifts to meet any other need they have.

If your church isn't meeting in person, find out how you can attend online. If they don't have an online service, you can join me and my church instead. Go to the website calvarynm.church/athome for more information.

Prayer

Dear God, I pray that you help me be a better friend to my family, my friends, and my work colleagues. Help me to stay socially connected when I'm unable to be physically present for fellowship or for church. I also pray that you help me realize which spiritual gifts you've given me and that you fill me with a desire to use them. I would also like to pray that you meet the needs of my friends today and that you comfort them during this dark time.

Day 8
Give Thanks

Scripture Reading

Therefore Jesus also, that he might sanctify the people through his own blood, suffered outside of the gate.... Through him, then, let's offer up a sacrifice of praise to God continually, that is, the fruit of lips which proclaim allegiance to his name. (Hebrews 13:12, 15)

Thanks be to God, who gives us the victory through our Lord Jesus Christ. (Corinthians 15:57)

Worthy are you, our Lord and God, the Holy One, to receive the glory, the honor, and the power, for you created all things, and because of your desire they existed and were created! (Revelation 4:11)

Don't be drunken with wine, in which is dissipation, but be filled with the Spirit, speaking to one another in psalms, hymns, and spiritual songs; singing and making melody in your heart to the Lord; giving thanks always concerning all things in the name of our Lord Jesus Christ to God, even the Father. (Ephesians 5:18-20)

Yahweh is my strength and my shield. My heart has trusted in him, and I am helped. Therefore my heart greatly rejoices. With my song I will thank him. (Psalm 28:7)

Give thanks to Yahweh, for he is good, for his loving kindness endures forever. ... To him who alone does great wonders, ... to him who by understanding made the heavens, ... to him who spread out the earth above the waters, ... to him who made the great lights, ... the sun to rule by day, ... the moon and stars to rule by night, ... who remembered us in our low estate, ... and has delivered us from our adversaries, ... who gives food to every creature.... Oh give thanks to the God of heaven, for his loving kindness endures forever. (Psalm 136:1, 4-9, 23-26)

In everything give thanks, for this is the will of God in Christ Jesus toward you. (1 Thessalonians 5:18)

Explanation

Well, those verses are pretty self-explanatory, aren't they? Give thanks! What does it mean to praise and give thanks to God though?

First, it requires a recognition that God is worthy of being thanked. You must acknowledge that God really did all the things the Bible speaks about. You must believe that God created the heavens, the earth, the sun, the moon, the stars, you, me, and everything else. You also know that God provides for every one of his creations. He gave us the earth and everything in it for our nourishment and pleasure. You hold onto the fact that God loves you.

You must believe that God himself stepped out of heaven to save you when he came to earth as Jesus. Trust that Jesus conquered death, sin, the curse, and your enemy Satan when he was crucified and resurrected. Jesus is worthy because he already won the spiritual war we're in. That also means you are victorious through him if you believe and have put your faith in him. You know that Jesus has sealed you with his Holy Spirit, the helper, and he is your shield and strength, especially in these dark times.

After you recognize God is worthy, then you must desire to worship him. That means you want to proclaim your allegiance and loyalty to him. You don't want to worship the world, the things in the world, or any false or foreign god. You want to devote yourself to Jesus and follow him and obey him with all your heart. You see, you love Jesus because of everything he's done for you.

So you sing his praises out loud and in your heart all day and every day. Everything you do is an act of worship and thanks to God. When you work, you work with all your heart because you know you're really working for Jesus. When you love, you love unconditionally because that's how Jesus loves. When you read your Bible, you thank God for leaving you instructions on how to be saved and how to live life, and for giving you promises, like eternity and heaven, that you can look forward to.

God wants your life to reflect how thankful you are for all that he's done for you. You see, when you form a habit of thanking God, your heart and eyes will change. Your heart will be full of love and your eyes will see God's light. There won't be any room for darkness anymore.

Lesson

Do you have a thankful heart that sings praises to God throughout the day? God is certainly worthy of your praise and words of gratitude.

Do you live your life in such a way that demonstrates how thankful you are to God? Living an obedient life that reflects Jesus's love will do exactly that.

Application

Today, give thanks to God! Thank him for creating you and all the wonderful things on earth that provide for you and bring you joy. Thank him for Jesus, for saving you from your sins and an eternity condemned to hell. Thank God that you, as a believer, get to live with him in heaven forever.

Throughout your day thank God for everything he's blessed you with in your life. Thank him for your family, your friends, and your church. Did you solve a problem at work? Thank God for helping you. Did the store have what you needed? Thank God for providing. Did you have food to make dinner and then not burn it when you cooked it? Thank God for being good to you. In everything you do today, give thanks to who it's all really due.

Prayer

Dear God, I pray that you take my current heart and replace it with one that's thankful and wants to sing your praises all day and every day. Please forgive me for being ungrateful. I pray that you remove the darkness that consumes me and replace it with your light. I want to develop a habit of giving praise. Please help me in this endeavor. Help me to see the good in all that you do and thank you for it. Put a song in my heart that'll lift my spirits.

Day 9
Be Joyful Through It All

Scripture Reading

This is the day that Yahweh has made. We will rejoice and be glad in it! (Psalm 118:24)

A cheerful heart makes good medicine, but a crushed spirit dries up the bones. (Proverbs 17:22)

Yahweh, your word is settled in heaven forever. Your faithfulness is to all generations. You have established the earth, and it remains. Your laws remain to this day, for all things serve you. Unless your law had been my delight, I would have perished in my affliction. I will never forget your precepts, for with them, you have revived me. (Psalm 119:89-93)

"Sing and rejoice, daughter of Zion! For behold, I come and I will dwell within you," says Yahweh. (Zechariah 2:10)

Rejoice that your names are written in heaven. (Luke 10:20)

I have spoken these things to you, that my joy may remain in you, and that your joy may be made full. (John 15:11)

Count it all joy, my brothers, when you fall into various temptations, knowing that the testing of your faith produces endurance. Let endurance have its perfect work, that you may be perfect and complete, lacking in nothing. (James 1:2-4)

Rejoice in the Lord always! Again I will say, "Rejoice!" Let your gentleness be known to all men. ... Not that I speak because of lack, for I have learned in whatever state I am, to be content in it. I know how to be humbled, and I also know how to abound. In any and all circumstances I have learned the secret both to be filled and to be hungry, both to abound and to be in need. I can do all things through Christ who strengthens me. (Philippians 4:4-5, 11-13)

Now may the God of hope fill you with all joy and peace in believing, that you may abound in hope in the power of the Holy Spirit. (Romans 15:13)

Explanation

You have much to be joyful about; therefore, you should rejoice! Happiness is good for you. It's medicine for your soul. Don't let the darkness suck you into its void. If you focus on the darkness it will drain away all of your happiness. You must control how you feel regardless of your circumstance by purposefully being joyful. Yes, you can control it because Jesus said you can. He's given you the power to do so – his Holy Spirit.

Be glad because today is another day. It's a brand-new day with wonderful possibilities.

Be happy because you have God's word in which you can delight in. His word told you how to be saved. It gave you life! So rejoice because your name is written in Jesus's book of life. You're already a citizen of heaven.

Be joyful because Jesus is coming to live with us here on earth one day. It's going to happen after the rapture, and after the seven year tribulation period.

Rejoice even in trials because you've learned that God uses them for your good. Trials and dark times test your faith. They give you an opportunity to demonstrate how much you love God and how strong your faith is. You develop endurance as a result. That in turn enables you to persist, persevere, and continue through whatever hardship comes your way. Be glad that the tough times are making you like Jesus because he was able to endure even up until death.

Rejoicing isn't just about feeling joyful or great delight, it has another meaning as well. It also means to give joy. You should be so full of joy that it abounds within you. That means it's overflowing and pouring out. You have an endless supply of gladness within you because, as a believer, the Holy Spirit lives inside of you. That's Jesus's power living in you! The darkness will go away, because you'll flood it with joy. And not just your darkness, but the cloud that shrouds your family and friends as well. While the world is fearful and full of anxiety about the coronavirus, let your joyfulness cast away the doom and gloom.

Lesson

Are you joyful because of all the wonderful things God has done for you? God wants you to be happy. He's blessed you beyond measure. Remember that you're a co-heir with Jesus. You're going to live in the most perfect holy place, forever. It doesn't get any better than that.

In the midst of dark times are you full of joy? Gods wants you to rejoice regardless of what's happening around you or to you because life here on earth is just temporary. Happiness isn't about circumstance, it's about eternity. Your eternal life is secure the moment you place your faith in Jesus. Evil and darkness can't touch you, so rejoice!

Application

Today is a new day. You're going to start afresh. Regardless of what happens today, you're going to be happy because you're going to think about how eternally secure you are in the hands of Jesus. Recall the promise from God that you identified on Day 3 and think about it today too.

You know, the devil wants to steal your happiness. Don't let him have the satisfaction! Instead, do something to counter his darkness and spread joy. Tap into the Holy Spirit and post pleasant things about your family and friends on social media, watch a movie with your spouse that you know will bring a smile to his or her face, or go for a walk with your kids and point out all the good things in God's creation along the way.

Prayer

Dear God, please forgive me for focusing on my dark circumstance that's drowning me in darkness. I pray that you help me focus on my secure eternal future where the darkness can't enter. Please help me be joyful through it all, so much so that it overflows within me and floods those around me.

Day 10
See The Light In Dark Times

Scripture Reading

We know that all things work together for good for those who love God, for those who are called according to his purpose. (Romans 8:28)

As for you, you meant evil against me, but God meant it for good, to save many people alive, as is happening today. (Genesis 50:20)

Casting all your worries on him, because he cares for you. Be sober and self-controlled. Be watchful. Your adversary, the devil, walks around like a roaring lion, seeking whom he may devour. Withstand him steadfast in your faith, knowing that your brothers who are in the world are undergoing the same sufferings. But may the God of all grace, who called you to his eternal glory by Christ Jesus, after you have suffered a little while, perfect, establish, strengthen, and settle you. (1 Peter 5:7-10)

God has now revealed to us his mysterious plan regarding Christ, a plan to fulfill his own good pleasure. And this is the plan: At the right time he will bring everything together under the authority of Christ-- everything in heaven and on earth. Furthermore, because we are united with Christ, we have received an inheritance from God, for he chose us in advance, and he makes everything work out according to his plan. (Ephesians 1:9-11 NLT)

"For I know the thoughts that I think toward you," says Yahweh, "thoughts of peace, and not of evil, to give you hope and a future." (Jeremiah 29:11)

Jesus therefore said to them, "Yet a little while the light is with you. Walk while you have the light, that darkness doesn't overtake you. He who walks in the darkness doesn't know where he is going. While you have the light, believe in the light, that you may become children of light. ... I have come as a light into the world, that whoever believes in me may not remain in the darkness." (John 12:35-36, 46)

Explanation

You can see the light in dark times because God works all things for good. Now, this is only a promise for those who are called according to his will. It's not for everyone. That means you must be a believer, someone who's put their faith in Jesus.

You can see the light in dark times because the evil you see in the world today and the dark times you're experiencing are being used by God for the good of other believers. Now, some of those believers might not be believers just yet, but they will be. When darkness comes, people who don't like it are drawn to the light. That's where they'll meet Jesus and be saved.

I read an encouraging email just recently from pastor Greg Laurie. When California locked down because of the coronavirus and churches couldn't gather in person, he had an unprecedented amount of people watch his weekend message online instead. In fact, online attendance increased 400% with over 230,000 people watching. Of those people, 1,438 gave their life to Jesus!

You can see the light in dark times because you know that God will perfect you, strengthen you, and give you peace since he's with you through it all. Your faith in Jesus is what withstands the darkness. You also know that you aren't alone in this war. Your fellow believers are dealing with similar difficulties.

You can see the light in dark times because you know God's plan. Today, the earth is under Satan's authority because we humans lost it when Adam and Even sinned. Satan's the god of this world. But you know that Jesus already won the war when he was crucified and resurrected, redeeming you and the earth! At just the right time, heaven and earth are going to come under Jesus's authority.

The best part of God's plan is that you get an inheritance because you've aligned yourself with Jesus. Everything will work out according to God's plan because God is faithful to keep his promises. God is in complete control.

You can see the light in dark times because you know that God only has wonderful thoughts about you. He has a plan for you. He has a future already prepared for you.

You can see the light in dark times because you believe in Jesus. He's the light of the world, and he's filled you with overwhelming hope. You no longer walk in the darkness because you walk in the light.

Lesson

Are you a child of the light? God wants you to put your faith in Jesus. He's the light of the world and the cure for darkness. Choose to believe, follow, obey, and love Jesus and you'll not only see the light, but you'll walk in it too.

Can you see God's purpose and his light during this dark time? God wants you to know his grand plan and trust in it. It should bring you great hope because, as a believer, everything truly will work out for your good.

Application

Today, think of your testimony and how you came to know and believe in Jesus. Perhaps you've known him since you were a child. Maybe you've only known him since this week. In either case, you used to live in darkness until you saw the light.

Think of how Jesus pulled you out of your prior darkness. Consider how he's kept you from the darkness all these years if you've known him a long time. Appreciate the people God put into your life that helped you meet Jesus.

Prayer

Dear God, I know you are faithful and trustworthy. Please forgive me for forgetting what you did for me in the past. I know that I can see the light in dark times because you've pulled me from the darkness before and you won't let the darkness consume me now. Help me keep my eyes focused on Jesus, the light of my life.

Thanks for reading this devotional. If you'd like to show your support for my work, please leave a review wherever you purchased this book. It's free to do, and it'll only take you a minute to write a quick sentence expressing your thoughts about the book. Your review is very important to independent, self-published authors like me. Internet and online bookstore algorithms favor books with reviews. They display in search results and at the top of search results more often than books without reviews. I even need a minimum number of reviews before I can purchase certain advertising. So, your review will help more people find this book. That will in turn help me sell more books, which means I can keep writing books for you. Go to rapture911.com/reviews if you need a link to where you can leave a review.

Thanks for your support!

Marsha

Read
Rapture 911:
What To Do If You're Left Behind

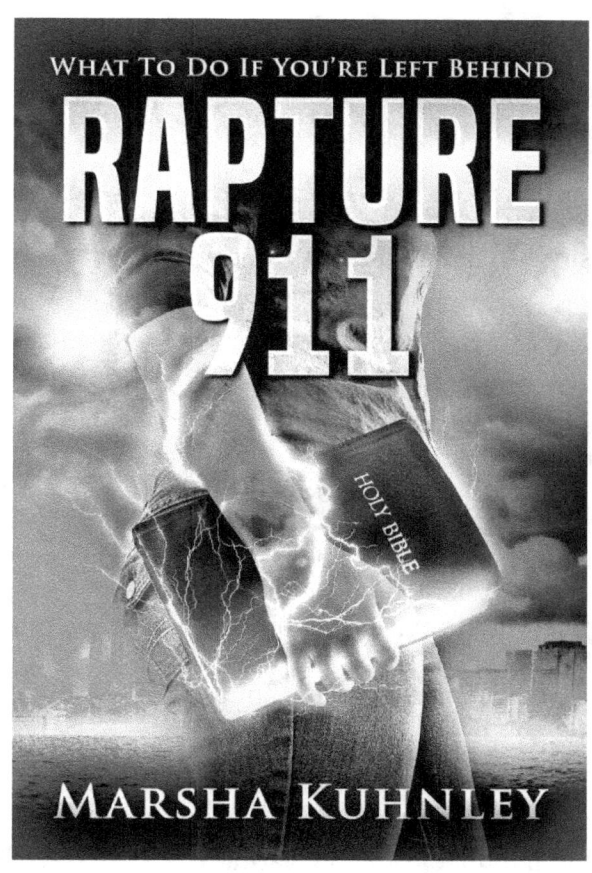

The End of the World is coming...

...but it's not what Hollywood portrays.

Are you uncertain about what God has in store for humanity? Do you fear for the salvation of your family and friends?

It could happen any minute.
The Rapture.

Will you be Left Behind to survive the Apocalypse? You can join the millions who will be saved.

Do you already believe? Then you can help those who are Left Behind. *Rapture 911: What To Do If You're Left Behind* is your all-in-one resource to survive the Tribulation and prepare for Jesus's Second Coming.

Inside this book is the following:
- Easy-to-understand Biblical analysis.
- Theological overview of forthcoming events surrounding the End Times.
- Why millions of people will disappear and what those Left Behind can do to be saved.
- The truth behind fake news and deceptions surfacing today that will be prominent after the Rapture.
- Examples of prophecies fulfilled that prove God's Word is trustworthy.
- Coping mechanisms from Biblical heroes to better handle shame, grief, and fear.
- A checklist of preparations, a handy glossary, and much, much more!

You'll love this handbook for navigating the Last Days because you want to live in Heaven and you care about saving your loved one's souls.

Get it now.

Books By Marsha Kuhnley

Rapture 911 Series
*Rapture 911: What To Do If You're Left Behind
Rapture 911: What To Do If You're Left Behind (Pocket Edition)
Rapture 911: 10 Day Devotional
Rapture 911: Prophecy Reference Bible

End Times Armor Series
The Election Omen: Your Vote Matters
The Election Omen: 10 Day Devotional

Other Works
Seeing The Light In Dark Times: 10 Day Devotional

Visit Marsha's website to find these books
rapture911.com

* - Also available as an audiobook

About The Author

Marsha Kuhnley is an American author of Christian non-fiction books. She has a passion for Bible prophecy, finance, and economics. She received her MBA in Finance and BA in Economics from the University of New Mexico. Prior to becoming an author, she enjoyed a career at Intel Corporation. She uses her education and career experience to take complex Biblical information and present it in easily understandable concepts. You'll benefit from over a decade of her research and study of the Bible, Bible prophecy, and Rapture theology. She lives in Albuquerque, NM with her husband where they attend Calvary Church.

Connect With Marsha

rapture911.com/connect

www.ingramcontent.com/pod-product-compliance
Lightning Source LLC
Chambersburg PA
CBHW052126110526
44592CB00013B/1770